H. MARSHALL GARDINER'S

NANTUCKET POST CARDS

1910 - 1940

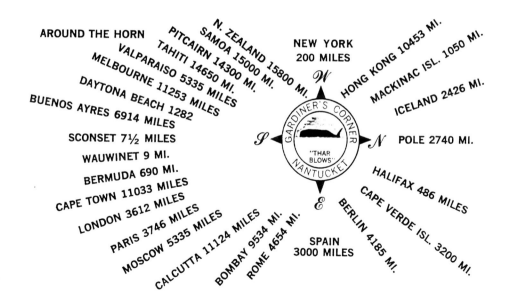

AROUND THE HORN
N. ZEALAND 15800 MI.
SAMOA 15000 MI.
PITCAIRN 14300 MI.
TAHITI 14650 MI.
VALPARAISO 5335 MILES
MELBOURNE 11253 MILES
DAYTONA BEACH 1282
BUENOS AYRES 6914 MILES
SCONSET 7½ MILES
WAUWINET 9 MI.
BERMUDA 690 MI.
CAPE TOWN 11033 MILES
LONDON 3612 MILES
PARIS 3746 MILES
MOSCOW 5335 MILES
CALCUTTA 11124 MILES
BOMBAY 9534 MI.
ROME 4654 MI.
SPAIN 3000 MILES
BERLIN 4185 MI.
CAPE VERDE ISL. 3200 MI.
HALIFAX 486 MILES
POLE 2740 MI.
ICELAND 2426 MI.
MACKINAC ISL. 1050 MI.
HONG KONG 10453 MI.
NEW YORK 200 MILES

GARDINER'S CORNER
"THAR BLOWS"
NANTUCKET

Geraldine Gardiner Salisbury

Acknowledgements

To all those who have shared with me through the years their knowledge of my native Nantucket and its history, I am deeply appreciative. I owe a special thanks to Mimi Beman for her valuable suggestions on publishing and to Michael Long for his technical input. I am particularly grateful to my daughter, Kit, for her dedication to this publication in the design and layout as well as her editorial expertise, and to my husband, Bob, for his support and encouragement throughout.

For the photographic and artistic legacy he left all of us who love Nantucket, I am especially indebted to my father, H. Marshall Gardiner, to whom this book is a personal tribute.

Library of Congress Catalog Card Number 94-93879
ISBN 0-9644037-0-6
Printed by Meridian Printing   East Greenwich, Rhode Island

First Printing 1995

Front cover: The Rainbow Fleet, Outward Bound

Frontispiece: H. Marshall Gardiner's Original Compass Rose

About the Author

Geraldine Gardiner Salisbury was born on Nantucket, the youngest of H. Marshall and Bertha Chase Gardiner's three daughters. Like her father before her, her childhood was divided between summer and winter homes, in Nantucket and Daytona Beach respectively.

Through her mother she traces her roots back to all but one of the first families of Nantucket and to some many times over. An artist in her own right, her mother was also an expert on the Nantucket hills, bogs, birds and flora, having grown up as a product of the Nantucket schools where an education included learning all about the island. Her scrapbooks of pressed leaves and flowers are still intact. Years of regular family "rantum scooting" across the island assured that the author would absorb some small fraction of her mother's vast store of familiarity with her island home.

Her early escapades with a Brownie camera did not lead to a career in photography, but in this book she has done what she can to preserve the work of her father, much as H. Marshall Gardiner's work itself preserved a Nantucket now gone by. In what seems to have become a family tradition, the author now divides her time between homes in Nantucket and West Virginia where she and her husband have retired from their respective practices of psychotherapy and medicine. In their three grown children and two grandchildren they have nurtured a "genetic" love of Nantucket, its ecology and its history.

In loving memory of my mother, Bertha Chase Gardiner

About the Photographer

Born in 1884, H. Marshall Gardiner first came to Nantucket in 1910, when he was 26 years old and the year-round population of the island was less than 3000. A native of Windsor, Ontario, his early childhood was divided between Detroit in the winter and Mackinac Island in the summer where his father was noted for his hand-tinted photography. By the time Marshall was 10 years old, Detroit was replaced by Daytona, Florida, a village in its infancy. W.H. Gardiner, Marshall's father, soon established a gift and photography business where his scenes of unspoiled Florida fast became popular.

It is not surprising that Marshall developed the talent and skills necessary to follow in his father's footsteps. Early in his career, he spent time in Bermuda where hundreds of his meticulously hand-tinted photographs of that island were sold over the years. Coming to Nantucket as an exclusive agent for Eastman Kodak, he bought 16 Main Street, heretofore used for occasional auctions, and established his photography and art supplies store offering the only on-island photo-finishing service. This soon expanded into a gift business and remained in the family for 51 years when Mrs. H. Marshall Gardiner sold the building to the Nantucket Historical Trust to be occupied by the Nantucket Looms. He designed and had painted the compass on the Washington Street side of the building, which includes the distances to both Daytona Beach and Mackinac Island. The spelling of Buenos "Ayres" was whimsically intentional as this was the name of the painter hired for the project. Though given a change of color and the current building occupant's name, this compass exists to this day as a beloved Nantucket landmark. Gardiner also had a gift store in 'Sconset, no longer standing, on the east side of the Gully Bridge.

In 1918 Gardiner acquired a little Quaker "cent" school building for a portrait studio, which he then had moved to the southeast corner of Washington and Salem Streets. He skylighted the north side of the building from roof peak nearly to the ground. H. Marshall Gardiner portraits are rare finds today. There is one gem on page 14.

Gardiner married two descendants of the original proprietors of Nantucket. His first wife was a Nantucket Macy. When she died after only eight years of marriage, he married Bertha, the daughter of George Coffin Chase. Coincidentally, Bertha's godfather was Henry S. Wyer whose photographs, post cards and souvenirs are also collector's items today. Wyer and Gardiner recorded the Nantucket of different eras with very little overlap, as Wyer was quite elderly at the time Gardiner's similar business was growing.

During his life on Nantucket, the summer season did not start until the end of June and was all but over by Labor Day. Although he kept the business going into October, Gardiner was afforded a good bit of time to work on photography. His winters were virtually free to pursue and perfect his craft until late 1934, when he took over the family business in Daytona Beach upon the death of his father, running it winters and the Nantucket business summers. He produced literally thousands of photographic images of the island, hundreds of which found their way into post cards. The surviving cards from which this collection of 189 is drawn record Nantucket as it was then and will never be again. His expertly hand-tinted photographs remain on walls across the country and his famous post cards exist in collections worldwide.

On December 4, 1942, at the age of 58, H. Marshall Gardiner died on Nantucket. He is buried there in Prospect Hill Cemetery.

About the Post Cards

For his copyrighted post cards, H. Marshall Gardiner engaged the same company his father used for his cards of Mackinac Island and Florida: the Detroit Publishing Company, whose patented process was called Phostint. While W.H. Gardiner began his photographic career using wet collodion negatives which required field processing, his son Marshall was able to use the newer and less restrictive gelatin dry plate. Location photography still required hauling out and setting up bulky equipment but field processing was fortunately a thing of the past. Roll film had also became available by this time and Gardiner took thousands of exposures on cameras of all available sizes and types. Still he maintained a preference for view cameras and large negatives as he required absolute clarity for the hand coloring to follow. Although Gardiner employed a variety of cameras taken from his extensive collection of photographic equipment, his post card views were initially taken on glass plate negatives.

It has been said that early scenic photographs are rarities because photographers found the cumbersome equipment too much to cope with and preferred the relative ease of studio work. Thus most early pictures are interiors. When the cameraman did move outdoors, it was to buildings and people close at hand. In Nantucket we are lucky to have had early photographers who ventured out across the rutted roads and sheep paths despite the physical difficulties in doing so, thus recording for posterity (albeit in black and white) our island of long ago.

Many H. Marshall Gardiner post cards were available in black-and-white as well as the more popular chromatic scenes. In some cases the subjects were the same, but there were some cards available only in black-and-white or only in color. Some views he would repeat in different seasons to show the changes in plant growth and complexion. A few examples are included in this book. Also interspersed here are a small number of Gardiner's "oil facsimiles" which were post cards that he embossed and textured with a shellac solution to appear like oil paintings. These he framed and sold for $1. They are distinguishable among the cards in this volume by their glossier, brushed appearance. Gardiner's hand-tinted photographs sold for $1.50 unframed for a 5 x 7, $3 for 8 x 10 ($4 and $6 respectively, custom-framed). Whereas these enlarged photographs were individually hand colored, all the post cards from which they were derived were mechanically reproduced and Gardiner gradually made more subjects available in that format. Occasional title misspellings from the printer may be detected, most notably where the printer "corrected" Nantucket's English spelling of Centre Street to Center. Gardiner also produced two panoramas of pond views and the much-copied 34-inch-long panorama of the town and harbor from Monomoy. Although notice of copyright was sometimes printed on the front of the card and sometimes on the back, copyrights were registered for all H. Marshall Gardiner post cards. The colors were subtle and printed on superior-grade stock unlike the gaudy, high-rag-content souvenir cards of the day. This alone attracted customers who recognized and appreciated quality. They were sold exclusively at Gardiner's for five cents each or six for a quarter, with less than two cents profit per card. Though the costs of producing the cards increased, the price Gardiner's charged the customer remained the same. When Mrs. Gardiner closed the store in 1961, she sold her remaining cards to one individual for one cent apiece.

All the pictures in this collection were carefully crafted on Nantucket between 1910 and 1940, but do not represent all the scenes once available. The Detroit Publishing Company went out of business during the Depression and with it died the excellent processing secrets unequalled in color post cards prior to the advent of Kodachrome. Around 1935, a former employee of Detroit Publishing set up the Photochrome Process Company in Philadelphia, assuring his customers he remembered the process and could duplicate it exactly. He could not. Hundreds of H. Marshall Gardiner post cards were printed by this new company; the difference in process is detectable. With the advent of World War II that company also went out of business. No more H. Marshall Gardiner cards were produced. They were immensely popular in their day and are still in demand today.

Landmark, Tristram Coffin Homestead

Tristram Coffin built his home near the head of Capaum Harbour along the north shore. He later built a second house on higher ground at the same location. Capaum Harbour closed to become Capaum Pond as a result of storms circa 1700. This landmark identifying his property remains today, partially obscured by shrub thicket beside a rough, rutted road.

Capaum Pond, North Shore

An Old Door

Front Doorway Jethro Coffin House 1686

The Living Room Jethro Coffin House 1686

"The Simple Life" Interior of Elihu Coleman House Built 1725

(*above* and *upper right*) Jethro Coffin was Tristram's grandson. His house on Sunset Hill is an historical treasure.

(*lower right*) The Elihu Coleman House remains a private residence on Hawthorne Lane.

BIRTHPLACE OF BENJAMIN FRANKLIN'S MOTHER   NANTUCKET, MASS.

Birthplace of Benjamin Franklin's Mother

PUBLIC LIBRARY   NANTUCKET, MASS.

Public Library

Ivy Lodge

(*above*) Ivy Lodge on Chester Street has now lost its ivy but retains its name.

(*upper left*) Behind this monument and horse trough on Madaket Road stood the birthplace of Abiah Foulger Franklin in Rogers Field.

(*lower left*) The Atheneum stands as it was when Maria Mitchell was librarian and Federal Street was still residential.

THE CUSTOM HOUSE   NANTUCKET, MASS.

The Custom House

Situated at the foot of Main Street, the former Rotch Warehouse, built in 1772, served as the Customs House during the Revolution and until 1913. The District Court and other offices have also been housed here. The elm tree in front, the first of a series planted along Main Street by Charles and Henry Coffin in 1851, was taken down in 1934.

Located at the head of Main Street, the Pacific National Bank was named for the ocean from which whalers made their fortunes. The success of the whaling industry provided livelihoods for candle-makers, coopers, sailmakers, ropemakers and many other related craftspeople. To the right of the bank stands the Methodist Church, saved from the Great Fire of 1846 by a shift in the wind. The post in the street was a "channel marker" for the new horse-less carriages. Placed at various downtown inter-sections, GO SLOWLY and GO TO RIGHT were printed down alternate sides of these traffic regulators.

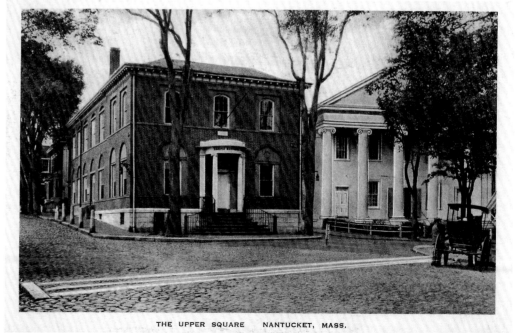

THE UPPER SQUARE   NANTUCKET, MASS.

The Upper Square

Liberty Street

A Gardner Street Door

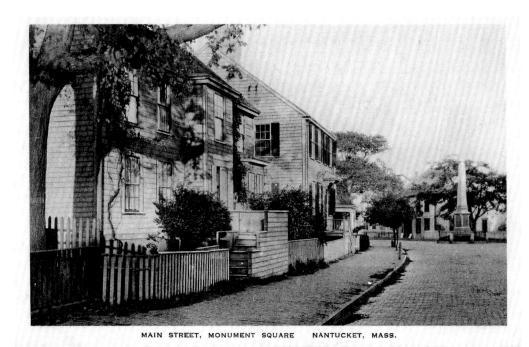

Main Street, Monument Square

(*above*) Built in 1835, 18 Gardner Street was the home of Captain Robert Joy.

(*lower left*) Looking east, the 1874 monument pays tribute to those Nantucketers who served in the Civil War.

Vestal Street

Many changes have taken place over the years on Vestal Street, site of Maria Mitchell's birthplace, built in 1790. As a child, Maria and her father William used the roofwalk to observe the stars. The Maria Mitchell Observatory, built in 1908, is used for research and is not now open to the public.

MARIA MITCHELL HOUSE AND OBSERVATORY   NANTUCKET, MASS.

Maria Mitchell House and Observatory

MORNING GREETINGS.   NANTUCKET ISLAND, MASS.

Morning Greetings

CENTRE STREET   NANTUCKET, MASS.

Centre Street

CENTER STREET   NANTUCKET, MASS.

Centre Street

CENTER STREET DOORWAY   NANTUCKET, MASS.

Centre Street Doorway

(*above*) 56 Centre Street was built in 1842.

(*left*) Centre Street when two-way traffic posed few problems. The Congregational Church, built in 1834, is shown more than 50 years before the new steeple was added in 1968.

A NANTUCKET THREE DECKER, FOLGER HOMESTEAD, CENTER STREET   NANTUCKET, MASS.

A Nantucket Three Decker, Folger Homestead, Centre Street

(*upper left*) The Peter Folger II home, built in 1750, remained in the family for nearly 200 years.

(*lower left*) One vintage auto chugs along in the distance.

(*below*) 5 Fair Street was built in 1820 by Frederick Chase.

THE ROUNDS HOUSE, FAIR STREET.   NANTUCKET, MASS.

The Rounds House, Fair Street

CENTER STREET LOOKING SOUTH   NANTUCKET. MASS.

Centre Street Looking South

AN OLD SALT   NANTUCKET, MASS.

An Old Salt

BOAT HOUSES ALONG NORTH WHARF   NANTUCKET, MASS.

Boat Houses Along North Wharf

ON EASY STREET   NANTUCKET, MASS.

On Easy Street

(*above*) The quintessential Nantucket fisherman.

(*lower right*) "Rest for the Weary Traveler" is offered by the sign at the BonTon Fish Market, John Taber, Proprietor. Closed early in the 1930s, the building was moved around the corner from this location.

The Skippers

The sign on the side of the Wharf Rat Club reads "Old North Wharf, C.E. Collins, Wharfinger." The Club began as a collection of Old Salts in 1915, who swapped tales at dockside by summer and around a potbelly stove by winter. A small cannon is fired to mark a member's arrival by steamship across the slip.

Killen's Wharf, as Straight Wharf was called in the era of these pictures, can be seen to the left where "coal, wood, ice and gasoline and water" are advertised on the roof sign. Old South Wharf, or Island Service Wharf, as it was known then, stands to the right.

Along the Wharves

Laid out in 1897, the Nantucket Golf Links (Wesco Golf Club) along both sides of Cliff Road has been gone for many years. Part of this land is now owned by the Nantucket Conservation Foundation.

Golf By The Sea

A Dandy Hazard, Nantucket Golf Links

Two women contemplate a ball lost among the lily pads in this murky water hole.

THE WHITE ELEPHANT   NANTUCKET, MASS.

The White Elephant

(*left to right*) The White Elephant which grew from three houses into an elegant waterfront hotel; the Auburn cottage, originally at #7 Cliff Road and moved by Dr. Ellenwood Coleman to its present location; the Breakers, a smaller hotel with cottages on Willard Street.

Demolished by its new owners in 1953, "Driftwood," the large home left of center and painted red, was owned by Mr. and Mrs. Clarence Gennett from 1912 to 1953. Originally erected in the late 1800s from two buildings, the earliest of which dated back to 1737, it was built on the site of the old Joseph Starbuck shipyard. The long dock and pierhouse in this picture fell victim to the hurricane of 1938.

BRANT POINT   NANTUCKET, MASS.

Brant Point

BRANT POINT LIGHT HOUSE   NANTUCKET, MASS.

Brant Point Light House

Brant Point Lighthouse stands as a sentry at the entrance to the inner harbor. The signal house in the foreground is now only a distant memory.

The Cross Rip Lightship, replaced in 1964 by a bell buoy, marked the half-way point between Oak Bluffs and Nantucket. Earlier versions of the Cross Rip met with disaster – one being lost at sea in 1918, with all hands aboard.

CROSS RIP LIGHT SHIP   NANTUCKET, MASS.

Cross Rip Light Ship

STEAMER ROUNDING BRANT POINT, NANTUCKET, MASS.

Steamer Rounding Brant Point

Arriving at Nantucket Harbor from New Bedford and Woods Hole, one of three sister ships sounds her whistle at Brant Point. Originally named Islander when launched in 1928, the name was later changed to Martha's Vineyard.

One gets a first glimpse of town from the deck of the steamship as she backs around the wharf.

BETWEEN THE WHARVES, NANTUCKET, MASS.

Between the Wharves

'NEATH THE BOW OF THE SKIPPER, NANTUCKET, MASS.

'Neath the Bow of the Skipper

Rainbows and other catboats set out from the slip.

The gangway at Steamboat Wharf provides a charming frame for the White Elephant and colorful catboats. The White Elephant and its cottages became a gracious waterfront hostelry. The building pictured was taken down in 1960 and replaced by the present structure.

THE WHITE ELEPHANT, NANTUCKET, MASS.

The White Elephant

1002 WHEN ROSES BLOOM, NANTUCKET, MASS.

When Roses Bloom

This picturesque White Elephant cottage was located on Easton Street.

NANTUCKET HYDRANGEAS, NANTUCKET ISLAND, MASS.

Nantucket Hydrangeas

On the Cliff overlooking the entrance to the harbor these hydrangeas once graced Lincoln Avenue.

Wisteria Lodge, Hussey Street

The tiny path of Bunker's Court was extended a few feet east to meet Hussey's Court. Together they became Hussey Street.

Hussey Street

Hollyhocks brighten this distinctive corner, facing east.

A Hussey Street Doorway

#7 Hussey Street, the home of Henry and Florence Lang at the time this picture was taken, was then named Wallflowers.

Quince Street

Quince Street, originally known as Crown Court, was opened in 1719.

NUMBER 5 QUINCE STREET, NANTUCKET, MASS.

Number 5 Quince Street

THE THREE GRACES, NANTUCKET, MASS.

The Three Graces

Bursting with a profusion of color in late spring and early summer, arched doorways were a fashionable touch during the time of these photos.

The Lattice Door

#11 Academy Lane, like so many others, lost its lattice arch to hurricane-force winds.

Ash Lane

Ash Lane is an example of the cobbled lanes and streets of old Nantucket.

A Little Bit of Heaven

Grandma's House

(*above*) Along fences, in window boxes and over trellises, flowers thrive in the Nantucket sea air.

(*right*) A glimpse of the Congregational Church can be seen behind the roofwalk.

Though laid out prior to 1800, and most of the houses along the lane built by then, a private academy erected at the southwest end in that year gave the street its name.

Academy Avenue

Where Sweet Flowers Grow

81493 JETHRO COFFIN HOUSE 1686, NANTUCKET, MASS.

Jethro Coffin House 1686

Prior to 1881 fire destroyed the kitchen of the Oldest House. These views show it circa 1910 and after the 1928 restoration.

This house and its grounds are now owned by the Nantucket Historical Association and open to the public.

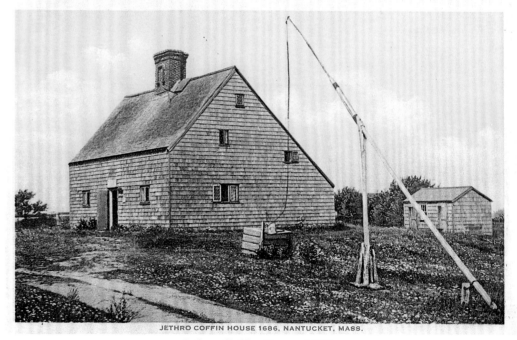

JETHRO COFFIN HOUSE 1686, NANTUCKET, MASS.

Jethro Coffin House 1686

1024   KEEPING ROOM, JETHRO COFFIN HOUSE 1686, NANTUCKET, MASS.

Keeping Room, Jethro Coffin House 1686

The Jethro Coffin House hauntingly transports the visitor back to the 17th century way of life on Nantucket. These interiors reflect the modest lifestyle of the early settlers. (*see also page 7*)

Large fireplaces were typical of the medieval English cottages built in early Nantucket, and were used for warmth, cooking, baking, drying as well as illumination.

1020   THE KITCHEN, JETHRO COFFIN HOUSE 1686, NANTUCKET, MASS.

The Kitchen, Jethro Coffin House 1686

A Memory of Old Nantucket

In the Slip

As commercial fishing replaced whaling, the vessels and wharves took on a different look. By 1915 hundreds of fishing boats entered or left Nantucket Harbor each week.

FISHING SCHOONERS, NANTUCKET, MASS.

Fishing Schooners

"SNUG HARBOR", NANTUCKET ISLAND, MASS.

Snug Harbor

The "Native," launched in 1924, was the first boat larger than a sailboat built on Nantucket since 1859.

The destination for Nantucket fishermen was Georges Bank in the North Atlantic. This meant voyages of only a week or two as opposed to the two- to four-year expeditions generally needed for whalers pursuing their quarry in the Pacific.

Getting Ready for Georges

Mending Twine

The ropewalks are gone from the scene but the art of mending, splicing and knotting was passed down to the next generation.

Wharf Scene

Reflections

(*above*) Steamboat Wharf was known as New North Wharf when it was built circa 1770. Lobster pots have replaced barrels of whale oil along the wharves.

(*right*) The last of the five wharves to be built (1835), Commercial Wharf is also known as Swain's Wharf.

Union Street Curve

Union Street, Looking North

Looking north towards Main Street, the brick building to the right housed the Town offices. Just beyond the Town Building facing Main Street was Gardiner's Corner, site of Gardiner's store and photo-finishing business.

Union Street

CHOPPING BOWL, NANTUCKET, MASS.

Chopping Bowl

(*above*) Located at 22 Union Street, Edward X. Ludwig operated this tea room in the 1920s and early 1930s while his wife ran the White Elephant Hotel.

(*left*) The house at 18 Union Street once stood at the head of Main Street where the Pacific National Bank is now. The railing and steps are from the Bank's earlier location on Federal Street.

Boone House on Union Street

Stone Alley

(*above*) The sandy path running along the back garden is Weymouth Street, now paved.

(*right*) Extending uphill from Union Street to Orange Street is a passageway known as Stone Alley. The bell in the clock tower atop the Unitarian Church tolls the hour in addition to 52 extra strokes at 7 a.m., 12 noon and 9 p.m.

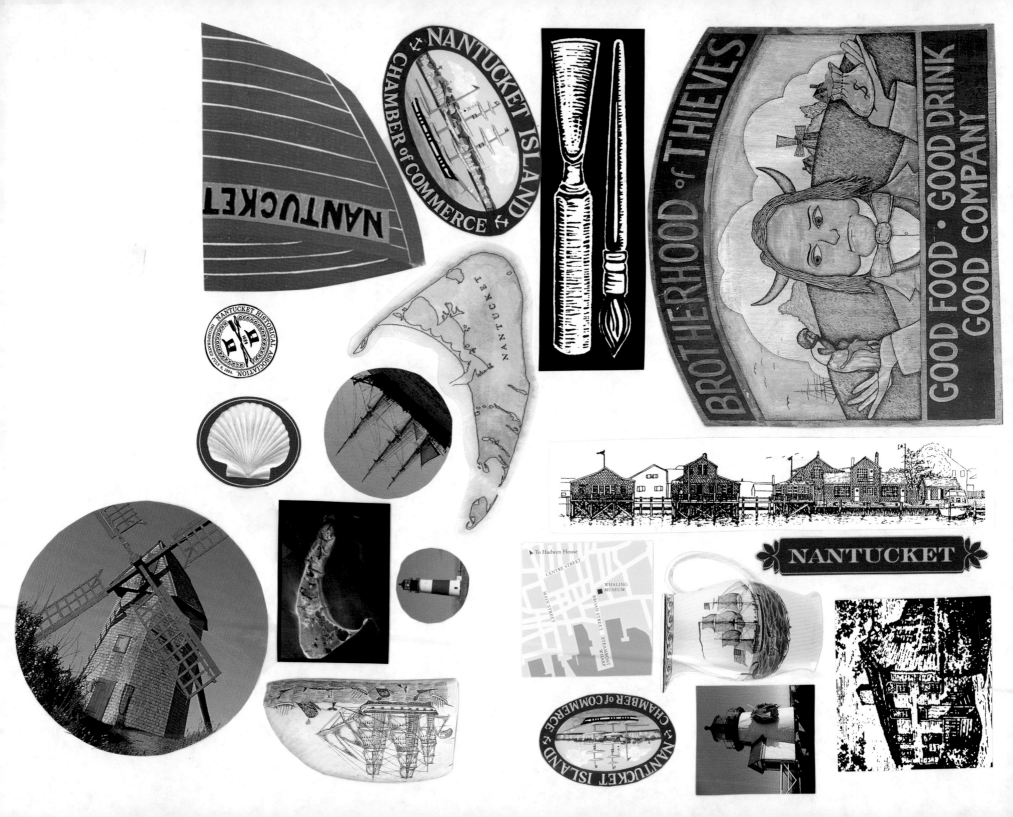

Tucked away behind the Orange Street mansions stands this 1755 gem obscured from passersby.

THE OLD UPTON HOUSE, NANTUCKET, MASS.

The Old Upton House

ORANGE ST. NANTUCKET, MASS.

Orange Street

Cobbled at the time this picture was made, Orange Street was known as Captains Row.

Sharp House

Stratton House

These homes on Gorham's Court provide a beautiful view of the harbor.

Flora Street

A Shady Lane

Mooer's Lane (*above*) was once called Judith Chase's Lane. Sitting at an angle to the street, her house was built in an area known as Fish Lots before the street itself was put in.

THROUGH HAWTHORNE LANE, NANTUCKET, MASS.

Through Hawthorne Lane

Built in the 1720s, the Elihu Coleman House is the only house from Sherburne remaining at its original site   In earlier days the profusion of mayflowers in this area drew eager Nantucketers after a long winter.

Many of the homes on the side streets of West Monomoy and Fish Lots, as seen in this card and the next, were built in the 1700s.

LITTLE COTTAGE DOWN BY THE SEA, NANTUCKET, MASS.

Little Cottage Down by the Sea

Little Gray House in the East

These once-small homes of mariners and tradespeople have been enlarged and changed through the years.

Fishing and sailing dories were practical small boats around Nantucket waters from the mid-1800s well into the 1930s.

Dory Mates

Prepared for launching, the catboat to the left sits on the ways. In the foreground the next boat awaits further attention before becoming sea-worthy.

Commercial Wharf

Resting on the gunwale of his dory, a fisherman mends his net beside an overturned pram.

The Torn Net

Early morning shows a quiet harbor while the fishing boats are at sea. The masts of a schooner can be detected along the far side of the wharf.

81555   SOUTH BEACH, NANTUCKET, MASS.

The Lifting Fog

THE LIFTING FOG, NANTUCKET ISLAND, MASS

South Beach

Fishermen's shacks and dories of the earlier days along this stretch of beach have been replaced now by more substantial housing and a town pier tethering pleasure craft.

43

FISHING BOATS, NANTUCKET ISLAND, MASS.

Fishing Boats

Catboats became as prevalent as commercial fishing boats in the harbor of the late 19th and early 20th centuries. Built different sizes, they were used for pleasure, fishing, sailing parties and "water taxis" between town docks and the north shore bathing beaches or town and Wauwinet.

81487   INNER HARBOUR, NANTUCKET, MASS.

Inner Harbour

QUIET HARBOUR, NANTUCKET, MASS.

Quiet Harbour

EVENTIDE, NANTUCKET ISLAND, MASS.

Eventide

(*right*) Well into the 1930s two- and three-masted schooners continued to make into Nantucket Harbor as working vessels, carrying coal, wood and other raw materials to Killen's (Straight) Wharf and to Island Service (Old South) Wharf.

A Quiet Day

Fishing shacks were utilitarian spaces to store gear before the waterfront changed and artists hung paintings in place of nets, blocks and tackle.

Fishing boats lay at dock five abreast. This was a familiar sight especially when a storm was expected.

North Wharf

81581   THE BOATMAN'S SHACK ON EASY ST., NANTUCKET, MASS.

The Boatman's Shack on Easy Street

The slip between North Wharf and Steamboat Wharf has been a scenic favorite over the years.

Railroad ties lie abandoned alongside rowboats hauled up tight. Narrow gauge railroad tracks lined the path that is now known as Easy Street. With the tracks removed during World War I and a bulkhead built, the railbed was replaced by a street in 1921.

81573   EBB TIDE, NANTUCKET, MASS.

Ebb Tide

81580 THE SKIPPER, NANTUCKET, MASS.

The Skipper

The schooner "Allen Gurney," built in 1867, made her last voyage to Nantucket in 1920. She was converted initially into a tea room and then a restaurant named the Skipper in 1921. Like so many landmarks of earlier days, she is only a memory.

Located on Steamboat Wharf, the Skipper was a popular dining spot for many years. One could choose the dockside dining room or chance sharing a meal with seagulls on deck under the awning.

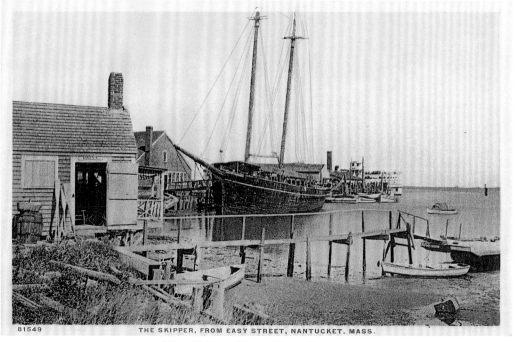

81549 THE SKIPPER, FROM EASY STREET, NANTUCKET, MASS.

The Skipper From Easy Street

1019   AN EASY STREET VISTA, NANTUCKET, MASS.

An Easy Street Vista

After the train tracks came up and the bulkhead was built, Easy Street became a superior spot for a view of harbor activity.

These are two of H. Marshall Gardiner's last painted photos to be made into post cards.

1021   TURNING INTO EASY STREET, NANTUCKET, MASS.

Turning into Easy Street

PACIFIC CLUB, NANTUCKET, MASS.

Pacific Club

(*below*) Three months following the repeal of the ban on automobiles in 1918, 94 of the "machines" were on island. Among the first, H. Marshall Gardiner brought an Overland across. Transportation by horse-drawn carts and surreys continued but dwindled by the 1940s.

81551   THE UPPER SQUARE, MAIN STREET, NANTUCKET, MASS.

The Upper Square, Main Street

(*left*) By naming the two prominent anchor buildings of Main Street Square the Pacific Club and the Pacific National Bank, 19th century Nantucketers paid homage to the source of their livelihood. The Pacific Club, formed by a group of whaling captains, has occupied the downstairs since 1854.

Wallace Hall, Main Street

72 Main Street was built in 1820 by John W. Barrett, prominent member of Nantucket's elite and one-time President of the Pacific National Bank. His wife Lydia is credited with saving their home by refusing to leave when it was destined to be blown up to prevent the spread of the Great Fire of 1846. In later years it was named Wallace Hall, the home of Mr. and Mrs. William Wallace.

Across from Wallace Hall, 69 Main Street was built in 1834, by Frederick Mitchell, also a President of the Pacific National Bank. The first brick home built on Main Street, it was later a home for retired Episcopalian clergy and known as Church Haven.

Church Haven, Main Street

NANTUCKET SHEARING CART AND QUAKERS, NANTUCKET, MASS.

Nantucket Shearing Cart and Quakers

Family transportation was most commonly by foot. However, those who had a cart and horse for work purposes could quickly convert it to a passenger vehicle for country excursions by the addition of chairs straight from the keeping room.

TOWN CRIER, MAIN STREET, NANTUCKET, MASS.

Town Crier, Main Street

A typical Quaker doorway, unpretentious and with practical sidelights.

A Quaker Home, Main Street

The family firebucket, always at the ready,
hangs by the door.

Grandma's Room

This well-appointed room suggests a family of some means no longer
rigidly adhering to strict Quaker standards.

Main and Pleasant Street

Main Street

93, 95 and 97 Main Street on the left constitute what are known as "The Three Bricks," the houses built between 1836 and 1838 by Joseph Starbuck for his three sons. He then used his influence to have Main Street cobbled the rest of the way from the Pacific National Bank to these houses.

94 and 96 Main Street were built circa 1845-1846 by William Hadwen, oil merchant, who married Eunice, daughter of Joseph Starbuck. They lived in the corner home and presented the one next door to their adopted daughter, Mrs. Hadwen's niece.

STARBUCK HOUSE, MAIN STREET, NANTUCKET, MASS.

Starbuck House

Summer Fêtes (given the old English pronun-
ciation "fate" on Nantucket) occurred in 1921,
1923, 1927, 1929, 1935 and continue, less
frequently, to the present.

81582

TOWN CRIER, MAIN ST., NANTUCKET, MASS.

Town Crier, Main Street

The town crier announces the opening of the
Nantucket Cottage Hospital Fête.

COLONIAL DAMES ON MAIN STREET, NANTUCKET, MASS.

Colonial Dames on Main Street

AFTERNOON TEA, MAIN STREET, NANTUCKET, MASS.

Afternoon Tea, Main Street

Nantucket Fêtes provide a look back at the grace of another era through tableaux such as this at the Hadwen House. In 1935, the author took part in a tableau of a "cent" school on the lawn of one of the Main Street homes.

Laid out in 1697, Main Street was called State Street until 1835. During the golden days of whaling affluence, small modest structures were replaced by the stately homes shown in these cards. Also reflected is the waning influence of Quaker austerity.

On the Way to Shearing, Main Street

The Macy Door, Main Street

Known as the Macy House, 99 Main Street is famous for its fan doorway.

81492 MOOR'S END, NANTUCKET, MASS.

Moor's End

"GOIN SHEARIN" MAIN STREET, NANTUCKET, MASS.

Goin Shearin   Main Street

In 1830, whale oil merchant Jared Coffin built Moor's End on Pleasant Street at the corner of Mill Street. Behind its walled garden were some of his tryworks which may have been the cause of Mrs. Coffin's refusal to live there.

A family leaves for the most festive occasion of early days, sheep shearing competitions. It was an annual event equivalent to the later Agricultural Fair as a community activity.

THE POND BY THE SEA, NANTUCKET ISLAND, MASS.

The Pond by the Sea

Shallop Pond, near Reedy Pond on the Cliff, was fast fading when Gardiner snapped this picture. It has all but disappeared in the present day.

Both of these North Shore ponds were close to town and near Washing Pond where the sheep were washed before shearing.

REEDY POND, NANTUCKET ISLAND, MASS.

Reedy Pond

59

GOLF BY THE SEA, NANTUCKET ISLAND, MASS.

Golf by the Sea

The golf links on the Cliff, developed in 1897, have now become a nature conservancy. Golf has been a popular pastime for Nantucketers over the past century. Presently there are three courses.

Through the centuries the North Shore has provided a choice spot for picnicking and safe swimming in Nantucket Sound.

"ALONG THE NORTH SHORE," NANTUCKET ISLAND, MASS.

Along the North Shore

A Peaceful Shore

The Road to the Spring

Autumn flowers add beautiful contrast to the sand and sea.

WHERE THE SEA MAKES IN, NANTUCKET ISLAND, MASS.

Where the Sea Makes In

One of the most admired of H. Marshall Gardiner's larger individually tinted photographs, "Where the Sea Makes In" still hangs on many walls on and off Island.

As the tide recedes, a line of seaweed and shells is formed along the beach ensnaring interesting bits of flotsam.

"THE NORTH SHORE AT SUNSET," NANTUCKET ISLAND, MASS.

The North Shore at Sunset

Birds skitter and dance through the sands where they nest. Human encroachment as well as storm damage remain a threat to the nesting places.

"WHERE THE SEA BIRDS NEST", NANTUCKET ISLAND, MASS.

Where the Sea Birds Nest

A WINDY DAY ON THE NORTH SHORE, NANTUCKET, MASS.

A Windy Day on the North Shore

The North Shore cliffs show a rugged coastline that changes shape gradually from the wrath of Nor'easters.

81488 MADAKET MOORE, NANTUCKET ISLAND, MASS.

Madaket Moors

The narrow dirt road to Madaket made for a slower journey best taken by horse and buggy. This was a prime area for blueberries, grapes, blackberries and beach plums.

This is the same location, only slightly further back, showing cart tracks in the foreground and a widening of the road to accommodate passing vehicles. Here the fall colors are beginning to invade the waning summer greens.

MADAKET MOORS, NANTUCKET, MASS.

Madaket Moors

Long Pond offers peaceful views for the traveler and a tranquil home for a family of swans just out of sight.

Twilight

Marsh rosemary, sea lavender and goldenrod co-exist with reeds along the north head of Long Pond.

A Nantucket Idyl

OUT MADAKET WAY, NANTUCKET ISLAND, MASS.

Out Madaket Way

The "crabbing bridge" though much changed today, has been a popular spot since before this early 20th century picture was taken. The road is paved and wider now but cattails remain a part of the scene.

The unspoiled sands of Madaket provide a safe home for seabirds and a spectacular view of the sunset for those in the small village.

81892   COPYRIGHT BY M. MARSHALL GARDINER, NANTUCKET ISLAND, MASS.

SAND DUNES ALONG THE SHORE, NANTUCKET, MASS.

Sand Dunes Along the Shore

The beach grasses and dunes provide protection for the birds and a hedge against erosion.

81860 SANDS OF NANTUCKET.

Sands of Nantucket

The Madaket surf has been popular with swimmers and fishermen but often risky, providing plenty of work for lifesaving crews through the years.

81490 SURF AT NANTUCKET ISLAND, MASS.

Surf at Nantucket

WHERE STILL WATERS FLOW, NANTUCKET ISLAND, MASS.

Where Still Waters Flow

Gardiner often photographed the same scene in different seasons to show the contrast of color. Here the spring-to-summer colors are in yellows, pinks and blues. The reeds in the far right do not show in the autumn picture below which was taken closer in.

The reds and lavender have created a different tapestry altogether.

WHERE STILL WATERS FLOW, NANTUCKET ISLAND, MASS.

Where Still Waters Flow

81583   SURFSIDE, NANTUCKET, MASS.

Surfside

Surfside, popular with surf bathers and surf-boarders today, is seeing a housing boom as well. In Gardiner's time Weeweeder Inn, a tea room and restaurant, was one of a half-dozen buildings in the area.

Ruts through the dunes, breaking down the vegetation, occurred less frequently in times gone by. This also grimly suggests shoreline lost to the pounding destruction of relentless Atlantic storms.

80888

ROAD TO THE SEA, NANTUCKET ISLAND, MASS.

Road to the Sea

Rutted roads, originally paths made by the Indians or grazing livestock, wander crookedly across the moors of chicory blue, bindweed and acres of waving grasses.

Road Thru the Hills

Saul's Hills, named for the Indian who lived in this area, has three small ponds commonly known as Poot Ponds, after the Indian legend of a whale (poot) seen rising here. The Geological Survey map "officially" identifies them as Foot Ponds.

Saul's Hills and Foot Pond

When he struggled to focus his lens on just the right spot, Gardiner could not have anticipated how the heather and bayberry would be replaced by houses within 75 years.

Sunset in the Hills

Sabatia Pond

Sabatia Pond, one of the Poot - or Foot - Ponds, creates a lovely oasis in the rolling heathland, home to the butterfly weed and Indian-posy.

The roses growing over Liberty Hall take the place of a backyard flower garden as that house, along with Mizzentop and House of Lords next, have only precious inches behind them on Front Street.

The Sentinels, 'Sconset

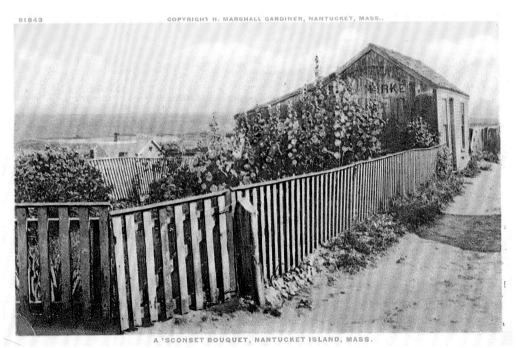

A 'Sconset Bouquet

An old fish market stands watch on Front Street with a coterie of hollyhocks.

Sunlight and Shadow, 'Sconset

Snug Harbor catches the afternoon sun through the trees. Next door Dexioma displays a splendid garden while, farther down, the old Gardner house runs roses up a roof trellis.

With rambler roses across the roof of Nauticon Lodge (*l*) and just starting over the roof at Auld Lang Syne (*r*), 'Sconset enters into the sunny month of July.

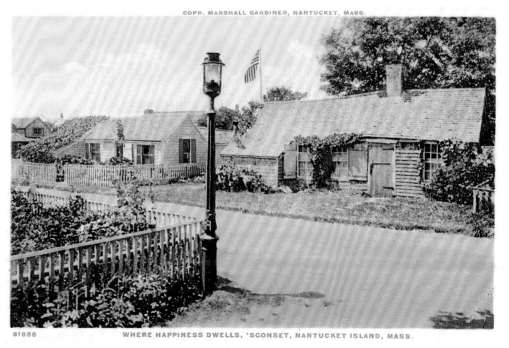

Where Happiness Dwells, 'Sconset

Auld Lang Syne, westside of Broadway and backing on Centre Street, is said to have been built in 1675. Its sagging lines attest to its antiquity. It has suffered periods of neglect during its long life but always manages to get resuscitated just in time.

Auld Lang Syne, 'Sconset

'Sconset Roofs

Looking south from Auld Lang Syne, Nauticon Lodge's wart is obscured by roses. These venerable neighbors have lived in harmony for 300 years. The 1770 Lucretia M. Folger house next down was bought and paid for with a supply of tea by the author's great-great-great grandfather Captain Peter Chase, sealer and Far East trader.

Nauticon Lodge basks in the morning sun. Climbing roses add the special 'Sconset trademark.

Nauticon Lodge, 'Sconset

Shanunga, devoid of its current hedge, is made up of two ancient dwellings. It has a colorful history as a public house run by Betsy Carey and, later, as 'Sconset's first post office.

Broadway, 'Sconset

Snug Harbor and Liberty Hall on the east side of Broadway are youngsters compared to Shanunga across the street which goes back over 300 years and has sprouted shrubbery and a hedge in this later view.

'Sconset Door Yards

Broadway in Rosetime, 'Sconset

On the left, Mizzentop hides behind roses. Beyond is the porch of Liberty Hall across from General Quarters. A close look will reveal five people in the distance.

Looking down Sheffield Lane one catches a glimpse of Broadway and a bit of the Atlantic Ocean between Dexioma and Low Tide.

'Sconset Bypaths

Heartsease fronts on the west side of Centre Street and snuggles back onto Shell Street, offering alternative spellings of its name on each street.

Heartsease, 'Sconset

Looking north from Main Street the hollyhocks stand where a barn was removed to the Gully Bridge and became the property of H. Marshall Gardiner. Next, the house known as Takitezie obscures In and Out, but a portion of the Corners peeks out from Pump Square.

CENTRE ST., SCONSET, NANTUCKET ISLAND, MASS.

Centre Street, 'Sconset

CENTER STREET LOOKING SOUTH, 'SCONSET, NANTUCKET, MASS.

Centre Street Looking South, 'Sconset

Centre Street, like the others, changed its appearance as can be seen in these two views from different decades. Along a rather primitive road, Ivy Lodge (*r*) has gone through several alterations. (*l*) Felicité, Nonquit and Driftwood turn their backs to this street.

78

81486 'SCONSET CORNERS, NANTUCKET ISLAND, MASS.

'Sconset Corners

The Corners, an unusual shape, stands at the north end of Pump Square, bounded by Shell Street to the west and Centre Street to the east.

Rounding the bend into Shell Street sits Castle Bandbox, followed by Clover Nook and Silver Shingles, facing King Street.

LOOKING NORTH ON SHELL STREET, 'SCONSET, NANTUCKET ISLAND, MASS.

Looking North on Shell Street, 'Sconset

CASTLE BANDBOX, 'SCONSET, NANTUCKET ISLAND, MASS

Castle Bandbox, 'Sconset

Looking south on Shell Street, the roses are only beginning to be trained to climb up the walls and over the roof of Castle Bandbox.

Castle Bandbox, in all its rosetime glory, was the first house in 'Sconset to have a fence. Here it is used as a prop for roses and honeysuckle.

CASTLE BANDBOX, 'SCONSET, NANTUCKET ISLAND, MASS.

Castle Bandbox, 'Sconset

The bluffs at Sankaty extended far out into what is now ocean. In the early part of this century the lighthouse had a secure foothold on the cliff. As this book goes to press, the lighthouse is in imminent danger of toppling off its once-safe foundation.

Sankaty Head, Siasconset

Looking Toward Portugal

The 'Sconset dunes lead to a beach from which Nantucket fishermen launched their dories for serious deep sea fishing. Their shanties above the bluff held little more than gear and "a cot and a pot." They eventually became the coveted cottages seen in these past few pages.

PATH TO SANKATY, SIASCONSET, NANTUCKET ISLAND, MASS.

Path to Sankaty, Siasconset

The pathway that led between the bluff and the houses no longer exists and the houses have been moved away from imminent danger.

Seventy-foot-high Sankaty Lighthouse was erected in 1850, on a rise of 110 feet. Its beacon saved hundreds of ships from foundering on hazardous shoals. Initially using kerosene, it was first lighted by electricity in 1933.

80332   SANKATY LIGHT, SIASCONSET, NANTUCKET ISLAND, MASS.

Sankaty Light, Siasconset

WATER HAZARD, SANKATY HEAD GOLF CLUB, NANTUCKET ISLAND. MASS.

Water Hazard, Sankaty Head Golf Club

These links are ranked the most difficult on Island. They certainly have the superior view.

The Sankaty Head Golf Club, exclusive then as now, was incorporated in 1921.

SANKATY HEAD GOLF CLUB, SIASCONSET, MASS.

Sankaty Head Golf Club

Sacacha Pond, former site of a group of ancient fishing shacks (later moved to 'Sconset) provides a calm area for swimming and small boat sailing from Quidnet side. Summertime brings Queen Anne's Lace, daisies and pipewort along the roadside.

SACACHA POND AND POLPIS ROAD, NANTUCKET ISLAND, MASS.

Sacacha Pond and Polpis Road

Gardiner used nearly the same scene to demonstrate the dramatic change of seasonal color. Autumn shows off the sea lavender, thistle and asters.

SACACHA POND AND THE POLPIS ROAD, NANTUCKET ISLAND. MASS.

Sacacha Pond and the Polpis Road

The Abandoned Road

Early in this century the barest vestige of a trail could be discerned behind this row of locust trees known as Harp o' the Winds. At that time no one seemed to know where the path had led - perhaps to a farm or an early track to Wauwinet. With the trees now indiscernible, the ghost of a road has vanished.

Out Pocomo Way

Pocomo is situated up harbor with a magnificent view spanning Polpis Harbor, Wauwinet, Great Point, Chord of the Bay, Coatue and down harbor to the town of Nantucket.

Only steps from the head of Nantucket Harbor lies the ocean side of Wauwinet. This starts the narrow spit of sand leading north to Great Point.

BEACH FLOWERS, WAUWINET, NANTUCKET ISLAND, MASS.

Beach Flowers, Wauwinet

COPR. MARSHALL GARDINER, NANTUCKET, MASS.

81857   SQUAM HEAD, NANTUCKET ISLAND, MASS.

Squam Head

Squam Head shows a rugged coastline tapering to Quidnet on the south and Wauwinet to the north.

A BIT OF WAUWINET, NANTUCKET ISLAND, MASS.

A Bit of Wauwinet

A dory sits at readiness.

Since before the arrival of the white settlers, the narrow sandy strip known as the Haul-Over has provided a shortcut for small craft between the calm of Nantucket Harbor and the open ocean.

THE "HAUL-OVER", WAUWINET, NANTUCKET, MASS.

The Haul-Over, Wauwinet

Great Point Light

This Great Point Lighthouse once stood a safe distance from the ravages to which it succumbed in 1984. The replacement is a replica as protected now as the earlier one had once been.

A furled sail rests in the stern of this sailing dory, waiting for the next high tide.

To the East'ard

Hidden Forest

Hidden Forest Trail

The Hidden Forest, located on private property and not discernable from the road, is lush with maples, tupelos, beeches and ferns. Wintergreen, bayberry and holly give cover to rabbits, pheasant and quail.

81844 WHERE WOODNYMPHS PLAY, HIDDEN FOREST, NANTUCKET, MASS.

Where Wood Nymphs Play, Hidden Forest

A magical glen, safe haven for cavorting deer and wood nymphs.

In Middle Meadow the ghosts of 18th century sheep blend in harmony with the bountiful heath.

A GLIMPSE OF THE SEA, NANTUCKET ISLAND, MASS.

A Glimpse of the Sea

90

Over the Moors to the Sea

(*above*) Mealy-plum vines mix with scrub oak, huckleberry and goldenrod to create a vivid palette of autumn colors.

(*right*) The ponds and wet bogs around Nantucket offer up flora with such appealing names as arrow-head, milkweed, silkweed, swallow-wort, pondweed and gerardia.

By Shimmo Shore

The Homeward Trail

A peek at town through the hills of Shimmo gives hope after an excursion out of town on trails such as this.

The Mill

Built in 1746, partly from ship timbers, the Old Mill's 30-foot arms outfitted with sails take good advantage of the brisk winds of Mill Hill.

A sight no longer enjoyed on Quarter Mile Hill, the Harp o' the Four Winds created a haunting foreground for sunsets.

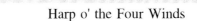

Harp o' the Four Winds

The Old Mill

The sun lowers over the one remaining mill of four that once stood in a row over 200 years ago.

AFTERNOON AT YACHT CLUB, NANTUCKET, MASS.

Afternoon at Yacht Club

The Nantucket Yacht Club, decked out in all its splendor at Regatta time, had been the sailing center of Nantucket less than two decades at the time of this picture. Austin Strong, then Club Commodore, introduced the use of small Beetle catboats in 1926 as safe vessels for children under age 17. His idea to dye the sails in different colors gave the Rainbow Fleet its name.

H. Marshall Gardiner arranged for this special outing so that he could photograph the colorful class of sailboats unique to Nantucket. Here they embark on a brief journey around Brant Point.

RAINBOW FLEET, NANTUCKET, MASS.

Rainbow Fleet

Rainbow Fleet Becalmed

Oops! As they were rounding the point in the channel the steamship passed and left a dozen young sailors tangled in its wake.

On their way once again, the Rainbow Fleet set forth to celebrity and recognition unimagined when these photographs were taken and hand-tinted in 1930.

THE RAINBOW FLEET, OUTWARD BOUND, NANTUCKET, MASS.

The Rainbow Fleet, Outward Bound

The Noon Boat Leaving Nantucket, Mass.